Where there is no leadership
The people fall.

—Proverbs 11:14

The Shipbuilder

Five Ancient Principles of Leadership

The Shipbuilder

Five Ancient Principles of Leadership

Jack Myrick

Fresno, California

The Shipbuilder
Copyright © 2005 by Jack Myrick. All rights reserved.

Published by Quill Driver Books
An imprint of Linden Publishing
2006 South Mary Street, Fresno, California 93721
(559) 233-6633 / (800) 345-4447
QuillDriverBooks.com

Quill Driver Books and Colophon are trademarks of
Linden Publishing, Inc.

ISBN 978-1-61035-255-0

First Paperback Edition

135798642

Printed in the United States of America
on acid-free paper.

Library of Congress Cataloging-in-Publication Data

Myrick, Jack.
 The shipbuilder / by Jack Myrick.
  p. cm.
 ISBN 978-1-61035-255-0
 1. Leadership. I. Title.

HD57.7.M95 2004
658.4'092—dc22

2004018855

Dedicated to
Fred Myrick,
a
wonderful man
And
wonderful father
who taught me how to lead
with my heart.

A very special thanks to Susan Campbell.
You gave this project the wings to fly!
Thanks to Chuck Harrison, who taught me it is
easier to learn by reading about others'
mistakes rather than by making them all myself.

Contents

Introduction

My intention was not to write a book. I had an experience. It was powerful and it changed my life in a wonderful way. After this experience I became passionate about sharing the information that had transformed my world leading others.

My wish for you is certainly to enjoy the story as it unfolds. I tried to share these principles in an interesting way. As the principles play out before you, you will notice that they are simple. They are easy to do. Yet knowledge without application is useless. They will only work if you do them and do them consistently. If you chose to go down this path, you will also find them highly impactful.

The people in your world are thirsting for a leader who cares about them and engages them in a way they truly feel valued as a person and a contributor. As you discover when you make these principles a part of your leadership behavior, people with passion can transform a team, an organization and a community . . . .

Carpe diem.

Seize the day.

CHAPTER 1

Marcus Fights Exhaustion

The tranquil sunset falling gently into the turquoise blue waters of the Mediterranean was little comfort to Marcus the shipbuilder as he struggled with a particularly heavy timber. His ship was only half-completed and he was weeks behind schedule. The booming trade business of ancient Greece created more opportunity for shipbuilders than could be met. Yet labor shortages, caused by distant wars, made it extremely difficult to find and keep skilled workers.

Dawn to dusk was a normal day for Marcus. With all his capital tied up in this current project, there was a good possibility he might lose his life savings, as well as his reputation, if the ship under construction was not completed by the agreed upon date.

After his calloused hands swung the hammer for the final time of the day, Marcus looked over the peaceful water. The last rays of the sun were sinking away. Sinking, that's how he felt almost every waking moment. No matter how hard he worked, he knew he would never finish this ship without more skilled workers to aid him.

He needed a team of forty strong men, but he was lucky if twelve showed up each day. The ones who did show up were lazy and seemed to lack any motivation. Marcus was mentally shot from pushing so hard day after day, and he was physically exhausted from the never-ending hours.

What to do? He had asked that question a thousand times with no answer to follow. Fatigue and fear were his constant companions.

Marcus sat thinking long after the sun had slipped beneath the horizon. As if the darkness weren't clue enough, the ache in his muscles told him it was time to go home. He would talk to his wife, Arayliss. She provided wisdom and guidance that he often relied upon.

Chapter 2

Arayliss Has a Suggestion

Marcus hung his cape on a peg in the corner of his small cottage. His wife and three daughters slept quietly as he removed some stew from a pot still simmering on the fire.

He ate in silence, until he felt a soft warm hand rub his tired neck. "How's my favorite shipbuilder?" Arayliss asked as she sat down next to her husband.

"Not so well. Only half my crew showed up today, and I feel it's impossible to meet my deadline, which means we will forfeit all our investment and profit. I don't know how we're going to make it," said Marcus in a concerned voice.

Arayliss took his hand in hers and said, "We'll make it. We always do."

They sat for a while just enjoying each other's presence. Arayliss was the first to break the silence. "Marcus, it seems your biggest problem is finding and keeping skilled workers. Is this correct?"

He grumbled in agreement.

"I've heard you mention," Arayliss said, "that this is also a problem for the other craftsmen and shipbuilders in Athens because of worker shortages." She thought for a moment and asked, "Is there anyone on the coast who seems to have solved this problem?"

He paused from eating his stew and looked up at her. "What do you mean?"

"I mean, it appears everyone in Athens suffers from this same labor shortage, yet, is there anyone you can think of who has solved this problem and could possibly give you some advice and guidance?"

"I don't know," he replied as he considered her question. They sat quietly for a moment. "There is someone I can think of who seems to have no problem finding and keeping workers."

"Who's that?" she asked.

"Barnabas, the master shipbuilder. He gets all the large contracts in Athens and seems to have an endless supply of extraordinary workers to help him. They say he's the best and busiest shipbuilder in the world. I guess if you are the biggest, it's easier because people want to work for you."

"Maybe he's the largest and the best because he knows something the others don't," she suggested.

Marcus thought about this a moment. "Maybe so, but he would never agree to see me. I'm his competition."

"You're very good at what you do, Marcus my dear, but I doubt Master Barnabas will feel your operation is much of a threat. Besides, you never know until you ask, and it can't hurt to ask."

Marcus lay awake that night worrying over his problems and thinking of Arayliss's idea to ask Barnabas for advice. Would Barnabas ever agree to see him? This was his last thought before finally falling to sleep.

CHAPTER 3

Marcus Bumps into Barnabas

Marcus was on the docks to start planning the day's work before the sun rose. The ship was starting to take form. The farther along they got, the more detailed the work became, and the more critical it would be to employ more skilled workers.

Julius, his loyal and trusted foreman, arrived shortly after Marcus.

"Good morning, Marcus. It seems we shall need some more short timbers and pitch if we are to continue today."

"Yes, I believe you are correct, Julius. I shall go to the market as soon as our crew arrives and they get started."

"I hope those who show up feel inclined to do at least half a day's work for a full day's pay," sneered Julius.

"They are all we have, Julius. Let's just do the best we can. I'll see if there are any potential workers at the market when I go to arrange for delivery of our supplies," said a frustrated Marcus.

The sun was well up into the sky before Marcus's scraggly crew started to arrive. By midmorning, only ten men had arrived. Quite depressed, Marcus decided to go to the market and take a break from his disappointment. "I shall return after lunch, Julius. Please get done what you can."

"Yes, Marcus, I'll do my best."

"I know you will Julius. That's all I can ask."

The market was busy as usual. As far as most of the known world was concerned, Athens was the center of the universe, and the market was the center of Athens. Goods from all over the Mediterranean were available to those who could afford them.

Marcus looked at the olive oil merchant and wondered if the ship he was building would ever carry any of the merchant's products. "That is, if I ever get it finished," he thought gloomily.

Maybe he should do as Arayliss suggested and try to talk to Master Barnabas. "Barnabas probably will decline to see me," Marcus thought, "but, as Arayliss said, it can't hurt to try. Yes," Marcus decided, "I will attempt to meet with him right now."

Lost in thought, Marcus bumped into a small elderly man who had stepped into his path. The older man lost his footing and fell to the dusty ground. Marcus leaped to the man's aid apologizing for his clumsiness. He helped the man back to his feet.

As the little man rose, Marcus's heart sank. He realized he had just knocked down the master shipbuilder Barnabas. Marcus stood there speechless and horrified. How could he be so clumsy? How could he be so unlucky? Barnabas brushed himself off and checked for injury. "I am fine young man, but you look at me as if I should have some mortal wound," Barnabas said, apparently confused by the younger man's expression.

"I'm . . . I'm so sorry Master Barnabas. Will you ever forgive me?" pleaded Marcus.

"It's already forgotten son, not to worry. Where were you going in such haste?"

"To find you Master," blurted out Marcus before he could compose himself.

"My, my. Your business must be of great importance to be in such deep thought and in such a hurry."

"It's a matter of life and death," replied Marcus.

Barnabas looked at Marcus with interest. He motioned to a marble bench next to the courtyard fountain. "Come. Let's sit, and you shall tell me of this most important business."

The two sat down and Marcus explained his situation and the difficulty he was having finding enough skilled workers. He then explained how his wife had suggested he seek Barnabas out for advice and possible guidance. Barnabas listened intently and patiently as Marcus completed his story.

"Will you help me, Master? Will you tell me how you do it? I am quite desperate."

Barnabas patted Marcus on the leg and said, "Things are rarely as good as they seem or as bad as they seem." He looked into Marcus's eyes and saw something that impressed him. He could not quite put his finger on it, but it stirred some emotion hidden deep in his past.

Barnabas stood and took Marcus's hand in both of his and said, "I shall give your situation some thought. I am not saying I will or will not help you, but I do agree to meet you tomorrow at this bench when the sun is straight up, if you agree."

"Yes, Master, anything. I will be here. I promise."

With that, Barnabas was gone, leaving Marcus sitting, his head spinning from the encounter.

CHAPTER 4

Barnabas Offers Marcus a Deal

The shock on Arayliss's face was apparent when Marcus recounted the day's events.

"How could you knock him to the ground?" she asked in disbelief.

"It was an accident but everything worked out fine because we meet again tomorrow."

"Sometimes an accident is not an accident," thought Arayliss.

Time seemed to drag on endlessly for Marcus the next morning. Julius knew something was definitely preoccupying his boss, but he had no clue what it might be. Marcus went to the market at lunchtime and headed to the fountain as agreed. He found Barnabas waiting for him on the bench enjoying the shade of a magnificent willow tree. The setting was tranquil even though it was right next to the market and all its haggling and commotion.

"Good afternoon, Master Barnabas," said Marcus as he approached.

"Greetings, my young friend. Please sit, and let's talk awhile."

Marcus sat and looked at the kind and gentle man who was before him. "I have considered your situation and have given it some thought," said Barnabas. "Your problem is a common one today in our area. It does, though, have some surprisingly simple solutions."

Marcus couldn't keep a look of bewilderment from his face. How could any problem so immense be remedied with simple solutions?

Barnabas continued, "Virtually every business today succeeds or fails because of leadership. I was taught five very important leadership principles when I was younger. I applied them in my business and became the most successful shipbuilder on the Mediterranean. I don't say this to boast, but to impress upon you the power of these five principles.

"If you learn them and apply them, you too can have great success. These principles are simple to understand, but you must never underestimate their power. Also, *simple* does not mean easy. It will require a change in heart and some very focused application. I am willing to teach you these five principles under two conditions. First, after you learn a principle, your effort in applying it must be 100 percent. Do not waste my time with half efforts. Is this condition agreeable to you?"

"Yes, Master. I will do whatever you say and give it my total commitment."

"Good. Now comes the second condition. There may come a time when I need a very special favor from you. If I deliver on my end of the deal and teach you how to solve your people problem, will you be there for me?"

"Marcus hesitated for a moment wondering what he could ever do for such a man as Barnabas.

"Yes, Master, I will be there for you if and when you need me."

"Fine. Now that we are agreed, are you ready to start your first lesson?"

Marcus sat up straight.

"Yes, Master, I am ready."

"Good," replied Barnabas. "Let me ask you, Marcus, what is your job?"

"My job, Master?"

"Yes, what is your job?"

"Well, I build ships, Master."

"Do you?" Barnabas asked.

"Yes," replied Marcus quite confused.

"This is your first lesson. Your job as a leader is not to build ships but to build men. Ships are just the by-product of your effort. The principles I will teach you work whether building ships, running an olive oil business, or managing a marble business. You see, as a leader, your primary job must be building people or your efforts are sure to fail.

"You cannot do everything yourself. You must have the help of others to accomplish your goal. Right now, you are focusing your time and attention on the manual tasks at hand. Even if you're really good, you can only complete a small portion of the job. If, through proper leadership, you can increase productivity and employee retention rates, you will receive a multifold return on your time. But this isn't all for your benefit Marcus. In turn, your employees will benefit from having an effective leader. Am I making myself clear Marcus?"

"Yes, Master," nodded Marcus.

Seeing some confusion still on his face, Barnabas started to explain, "I know right now, you must work physically because you are shorthanded, but you must understand your job as a leader is . . . well, let me describe it. Picture your fine ship upon completion. As the leader, you represent the tiller. Your men and crew represent the ship and all its components. Together you can accomplish great things. You can go to wonderful exotic places. You only lack one thing to make this happen."

"What's that?" asked Marcus.

"Wind. Wind, my friend. You need the gentle blowing of the wind to move you to where you want to go. It is the one ingredient you now lack. We must find your wind. And together, I believe we can find it. Marcus, just like the real wind, this one missing ingredient is not seen but felt. Are you ready to begin the journey to find your wind?"

"Yes, Master. I am ready."

"Good. Let me see your hand, Marcus."

Marcus extended his hand for Barnabas to examine. "Look at your hand. It has five fingers. Each finger by itself has little strength."

Barnabas then formed his hand into a fist. "If I take all five fingers and form them into a fist, they become a weapon that can crush a mighty foe.

"The principles you are to learn are the same way. They hold strength standing alone, but together they form a mighty force. Today, you shall learn the first of the five principles. Each principle will be practiced for one week before proceeding on to the next one. You must not question the principle, because any doubts you have will soon be erased."

Barnabas reached into his leather bag and removed a small box. When he opened the box, Marcus saw that it contained five clay tablets. Barnabas removed a tablet-marked "Principle Number I" and handed it to Marcus.

"You are about to take a journey. It is a journey of discovery. I, too, was taught these principles as a young man. I have applied them and prospered more than I could have ever imagined. More important, I have discovered true happiness from leading and helping others. Please read to me what the tablet says."

Marcus read silently then out loud,

"Make them feel appreciated."

Puzzled, Marcus asked, "What does it mean, Master?"

"It means that one of the greatest needs we have as a person is to be appreciated. As a leader, our job is to make sure those working for us have that need met by us. If you can make each and every one of your crew feel appreciated and significant, you will go a long way to solving your worker shortage. Pretend each person that works for you has a sign around their neck that reads, 'Make me feel important.'

"You cannot fake this; your men will know. It must come from your heart. Each and every person working for you right now can choose to work anywhere in Athens. What's important is that they choose you. Let them know how much you truly appreciate all their hard work and effort. Make a conscious effort today and during the rest of the week to instill this feeling in the people around you. Read

PRINCIPLE NUMBER I

MAKE THEM FEEL APPRECIATED

this tablet three times a day during a quiet moment. By the end of the week, it should be at the top of your mind.

"Marcus, you must make a commitment to yourself that you will do this and do this sincerely."

"Yes, Master, I will do as you say."

"Good, meet me here next week at this time to report your progress on principle number one. Then we will discuss the secret of principle number two."

CHAPTER 5

Marcus Shows His Appreciation

As he headed back to the dock, Marcus thought, "How could he appreciate these guys when half of the time he felt like killing them?" He decided to really give it a try. His way was not working, so he had nothing to lose.

On his way back through the market, Marcus picked up some melons that had been chilling in spring water. The sun was blistering when he returned to the ship. Working with pitch was a hot and nasty job. Everyone hated this part of the shipbuilding process. He called the men over to the shade of a nearby tree and began cutting the melon. The men were hot and sticky. The cold melon was an instant hit.

"Thank you for the melon," spoke Julius. All the men nodded.

"I know how hard you work, and this is just a little something to say thank you. I really do appreciate all your hard work and effort." The men looked back and forth at each other with mild confusion and surprise, and then smiled as they finished their melon.

The rest of the day went smoothly. There was none of the petty bickering and fighting that usually accompanies a ship's construction site.

"I'm leaving now," said Julius, as he wiped the last bit of tar from his hands.

"Julius, come here a moment, please," said Marcus. "Julius, you are my right arm. We have worked together a long time. When people work that long together and as close as we have, one often will take the other person's efforts for granted. I just wanted to take a moment and tell you how important you are to me as a friend and coworker. My life is much richer because you are in it. I just wanted to tell you that and to say thank you. I truly appreciate all you do." Marcus shook Julius's hand and said, "Now come along, let's go see our families."

Arayliss had supper ready upon Marcus's arrival. And, to his delight, the children were still awake. The family enjoyed their meal, then Marcus put the girls to bed with a story. *The Odyssey* was a tale becoming popular around town.

"Tell me," Arayliss said, as the two sat watching the stars. "How was your day?"

"Good," said Marcus.

"Women are not like men," she shot back. "'Good' will not do at all. I want details, lots of them. Tell me everything," she said as she moved her chair closer.

Marcus described the events of his day and produced the tablet marked "Principle Number I."

"Make them feel appreciated," she read out loud. "Do you think it will work?"

"I don't know. The day went smoothly, and the men seemed happy. The strangest part was when I spoke to them, I really did mean what I said. I just haven't thought about telling them because I'm so busy, and I just assumed they knew I appreciated them."

She took his hand and looked into his dark piercing eyes, "Each night before we go to sleep, you tell me you love me. You don't have to do that, but it makes me feel good," said Arayliss.

"You're right. They need to know how much I appreciate them." He squeezed her hand and said, "I love you."

She smiled, kissed him, and said, "I love you too."

CHAPTER 6

Marcus Notices a Change Brewing

Julius beat Marcus to the shipyard the next day. "Good morning, Master."

"Good morning to you, Julius. What brings you in so early?"

"Oh, I just wanted to get a jump on things," replied Julius.

To Marcus's surprise, several other men arrived early. By the beginning of the shift, most men were at the yard. To his amazement, Marcus had a crew of sixteen for the entire day.

As promised, Marcus read his tablet three times that day. He made it a point to work one-on-one with each man at some time during the day. He also imagined that each man had a sign on his neck which read, *"Make me feel important."*

Marcus looked for ways to show his gratitude and found himself enjoying his work more and more as time passed.

The days went quickly, and Marcus read his tablet often as a reminder of the first principle, *"Make them feel appreciated."* By the end of the week his crew had grown to eighteen, and all were showing up for work regularly.

Marcus's attitude was contagious, and there was a noticeable change in the atmosphere around the uncompleted ship. Marcus was tempted to be hopeful, but he quickly realized how far they had to go.

CHAPTER 7

The Two Rubies

The beginning of the week found Marcus pacing in front of the marble bench. He was anxious and nervous about his next lesson. When Barnabas arrived, he sat and listened to Marcus review the week's activities.

"I did as you said, Master, and by the end of the week we had eighteen workers showing up! I see progress, but I just hope it is not too late."

"Relax, my son. Athens wasn't built in a day. The fruit from the changes you are making in how you approach your men needs time to mature. It sounds like you are making good strides though."

"I have a question, Master. I tried hard to praise and appreciate each man, but there were times when they did things that were just wrong. Am I to ignore this?" asked Marcus.

"Your job as a leader is to build men. To build men, you must maintain discipline and insure the quality and integrity of your project. You don't overlook these situations, but use them as opportunities for training and growth. This brings us to principle number two."

Barnabas removed the box from his sack and opened it. Inside were slots for the five tablets. "May I have tablet number one Marcus?" Marcus handed it to Barnabas who placed the tablet in its proper slot. He then removed the tablet marked Principle Number II. "Marcus, please recite principle number one."

"Make them feel appreciated," said Marcus.

"Splendid. I want you to know that as you proceed to principle number two, you are not to stop practicing principle number one. These principles are the building blocks of your leadership success. You do not replace one with another but build one upon the other. Is that clear?"

"Yes, Master."

"Fine. Please read me what is on tablet number two."

"See their potential, not their flaws."

PRINCIPLE NUMBER II

SEE THEIR POTENTIAL, NOT THEIR FLAWS

Before Marcus could say anything else, Barnabas held up a rough stone and handed it to Marcus.

"What do you have in your hand?"

Marcus examined the odd-looking red stone in his hand. "It's a red-looking rock, Master." Marcus placed the stone on the bench between them.

Barnabas then took out a cut and polished ruby. He held it up to the light and let the sun sparkle through it, showing off the stone's beauty. "This is one of the most magnificent stones in Athens." He tossed it to Marcus who almost dropped the stone as it bounced off his hand and into his lap. Barnabas laughed and asked Marcus to examine both stones again. "What is the difference between the two stones, Marcus?"

"Well, one seems to be a red rock and the other an exceptional gem. One is valuable, the other is not, I guess."

Barnabas replied, "On the contrary, son. The rough stone you so casually placed on the bench is soon to become the most valuable ruby in all Greece. It is a ruby of the finest quality. All it lacks is to be in the hands of a master jeweler. Once he takes the rough edges off and applies some polish, the world will see how beautiful the stone can truly be.

"People are the same as this rough stone, my friend. Put in the hands of a master, they too can become more than the eye can at first perceive. It takes the vision and the skill of a master leader to bring them to their full potential.

"Look at the men on your crew. With your guiding hand, they can each become much more than the eye sees. It will take your hand to guide them and chip away the rough edges. Always see them as they will become, not as they are."

"I understand," said Marcus.

"Good, go to work. Same time next week." Barnabas patted Marcus on the back and then disappeared into the market.

CHAPTER 8

The Men Feel the Change Brewing

Walking back to the shipyard, Marcus started to think of his men one at a time. Marcus knew Julius was a fine man and would someday be his own shipbuilder. He suddenly felt responsible to help him achieve this. He then went down his list of crew, one by one, and tried to imagine their individual potentials. He remembered the illustration of the two rubies and tried to imagine each man on his crew as a priceless gem with some rough edges to be worked off.

He started to become excited and a little proud of what might be accomplished, if he could just figure out how to help these men reach their potential. Marcus, for the first time, began to see his job as a leader—as someone to bring out his men's potential instead of plowing through the shipbuilding process.

Marcus's men saw and felt a change in Marcus and worked harder to please their newly inspired leader.

CHAPTER 9

Marcus Learns the Value of Influence

Barnabas listened patiently as Marcus described the events of the previous week. He now had twenty-five men showing up every day and three more prospects coming to see him early this week. Marcus's men started to believe both they and their work were important. Word started to go around that there was something different, something special about Marcus and his crew.

"I tried to look at each man as an individual and then determine his strengths. I soon found I had some men in the wrong positions. I made some changes and explained to them why I felt this was a wise move, and, before I knew it, our productivity increased.

"Barnabas, when I talked to each man about his strengths and future potential, he began to take pride in his work and seemed to excel even more. I have looked at my current crew and feel that this can quite possibly be the best team on the coast—if I can just work with them to develop their abilities a little more."

Barnabas smiled as he listened to his student believing that Marcus was well on his way to mastering principle number two. After Marcus had finished his account of the week, they sat in silence for a while and watched the people of Athens buzzing around the market like bees around a hive.

"Master, may I ask you a question?"

"Certainly," said Barnabas.

"Master, how did you come to learn these five principles of leadership?"

"Back more years than this old man cares to remember, I was a poor struggling worker on a shipbuilding crew. I was coming home late from an exhausting day of work and came upon four bandits attacking a man at the edge of town. On impulse, I picked up a stick and started screaming as I ran toward the beaten man. I surprised the bandits so much they stopped and fled into the darkness. I looked down to see that the man was bleeding from a wound on his head. He was unconscious. I carried him to my small hut, and I cleaned his wounds and let him rest the night. He awoke the next day.

"I put him at ease, told him he was safe, and described to him the last evening's events. I remember he was grateful and appreciative. He seemed to be such a kind and gentle man that my blood boiled at the thought of those rogues and their cowardly deed. He tried to pay me a reward. I flatly refused and saw him off that afternoon.

"A week later, I heard a knock at the door and to my surprise my injured friend stood before me. He was dressed in the finest silks and had an entourage of loaded camels and armed soldiers."

"'Hello, my mighty rescuer,' he said.

"'Hello,' I replied while trying to absorb the mass of wealth before me.

"'I hope I am not intruding.'

"'No sir. Please come in.'

"We sat at my old hard, wood table.

"'I'm on my way to Crete and wanted to stop by on my way out of town. I would like, with your permission, to present you with a small but priceless gift,' said my visitor.

"'Sir,' I replied, 'I do not expect or feel worthy of money. Your well-being is reward enough for me.'

"The visitor replied, 'I thought you might say that, being a man of your character. Please let me continue then you can decide.'

"I found him a little wine and some cheese. He ate and then continued.

"'Barnabas, I am one of the most successful merchants on the Mediterranean. One of the reasons for my success is that I have the ability to see potential in people, even if it is not obvious to them or others around them. When I met you, I soon determined you have all the qualities to become a great leader. You just need to develop this talent. The gift I want to give you is not money but knowledge.'

"He removed a small box from his shoulder bag and showed me the contents.

"'Barnabas, inside this box are five tablets and on each tablet is a principle for great leadership. They were passed on to me by a great man a long time ago. I have learned these principles and practiced them every day of my life. I owe all I possess in wealth and happiness to their power. As they were passed to me so long ago, I now wish to pass them on to you and request that, as a favor to an old man, you accept them and use them to achieve great things in your life.'

"I took the box as he handed it to me, not knowing what to say. He smiled with tears forming in his eyes. I knew, without explanation, that this was a very important moment in both of our lives. He placed his hand on my cheek and thanked me.

"Then he said, 'I wish I could stay and tutor you, but my business takes me far away. I have written down the steps to learning and applying the principles. I am sure you will discover how to best employ them in your own life and work. I wish you great success and happiness, Barnabas.'

"He hugged me like a proud father would and left. I never saw him again. I took the tablets and applied them to my life with serious commitment and diligence. In turn, I have achieved more than I ever imagined. Not a week goes by that I don't read a tablet and apply my time and energy on the principle written.

"Enough with the past, we must get to principle number three, hopefully, before the sun sets."

Barnabas opened the box. He replaced tablet number two and handed Marcus tablet number three. Marcus read it out loud,

"Lead with influence, not power."

Marcus then asked, "Are they not the same, Master?"

"No, not at all," Barnabas said. "They are quite different. Let me try to explain. Power is when you force your will upon people whether they like it or not. They do what you want them to do because of your position, which allows you to grant or withhold rewards or, in some instances, mete out punishments.

"Influence is when you express your will and people accept and comply with your wishes freely.

PRINCIPLE
NUMBER III

LEAD WITH
INFLUENCE,
NOT POWER

"Power, as in the government or military, can be assigned or transferred. Influence, on the other hand, comes from earning devotion and allegiance.

"All great things in this world are achieved by people with influence. They lead and others follow."

"How do I earn this influence with people, Master?"

"Practicing the principles of tablet number one and tablet number two is a great foundation. And, always remember that people do as they see, not as they are told. You must model the message. Lead people by example.

"Influence is all about who you are as a person, your character, your integrity. Power can be bought and sold, but influence, as I said, must be earned. Using the first two principles, focus this week on leading your men with influence, not power."

Marcus thought for a moment then asked, "Does this mean I will never exercise the power of my position?"

"No, Marcus. There will be times when you must use the power of your position, but only because your influence has broken down.

"I know this is hard to grasp at first. Just remember that this whole process of learning to lead with influence is a transformation, a change of heart, if you will. Some make this transition easily, with others it takes more time. Regardless, leadership, in its best and purest form, operates through influence, not power."

"I think I understand, Master."

"Good," said Barnabas as he rose. "Go to work now. Your time is running short. We shall meet again next week to see how my star pupil has progressed."

CHAPTER 10

Immediate Respect

Marcus was in deep thought as he made his way back to the ship. His mind was on the task at hand and not on the shouting shopkeepers bargaining their wares of oil, wine, glass, and countless other curiosities sold in the market of Athens.

As Marcus walked over the rocky hill, the turquoise water of the Mediterranean presented itself. He saw the ship in the distance and started to worry that he had only four weeks left until his agreement came due.

He did not know who the ship's buyer was, but he knew Mathis, the ship's purchasing agent, was not a forgiving soul and would impose the maximum penalty if the ship was not completed on time.

The men seemed happy at his return, and he was quite pleased with Julius who had hired three new workers in his absence. This made his crew thirty-two men deep, more than he had ever employed.

A crew of forty was his goal, but both Marcus and Julius were amazed at the progress their crew had made in two weeks.

"We might make it yet," Marcus thought to himself.

Marcus had little time to worry during the following week. New workers meant extra training. He worked each day trying to lead through his influence, and he exercised his power only when necessary.

The only problem he had was that he felt the new men must prove themselves and earn his respect before he applied the first three principles with them, and Marcus had not seen enough of this so far.

He must remember to ask Barnabus about the new men's responsibility to respect him and to accept his influence as a leader from Day One, so he could work better to develop them. Applying these principles of Barnabas's before these things happened seemed to go against the normal notions of leadership.

CHAPTER 11

Unearned Love

At the beginning of the week, Marcus found Barnabas sitting on their bench eating a basket of figs and bread.

"Sit, my friend. Eat some lunch, and tell me about your week."

Marcus sat and enjoyed a few of the figs. "Master," Marcus asked in between bites, "I have done as the tablets say for the last three weeks and have seen dramatic improvement in my situation. I truly appreciate all my crew does and work hard to make them know and feel this. I also look at each man individually and seek his potential and focus on his strengths. I do both of these activities while trying to lead through my influence. The result of all this is I now have thirty-two workers, and I am possibly in a position to meet the scheduled completion date. I am starting to feel very good about my crew.

"Yet, I am having a problem with the first three principles with the newer men. I am feeling hesitant about applying the principles to the newer men until they have proven their loyalty and worthiness."

Barnabas smiled and handed Marcus tablet number four and replaced tablet number three in the box with the others. "I used to feel the same way until I started to live my life according to principle number four. Please read it out loud, Marcus."

"Love them first,"

read Marcus.

"I don't understand. Please explain, Master."

"When we talk about love, Marcus, we are not talking about emotional love, not the feeling of love, but the act of love.

"It's how we decide up front to treat people. We decide before the person even earns it. We decide that we will treat them with compassion and respect even before we know them. They do not have to earn this from us. By doing this, we actually speed up a relationship that enables us to lead them with influence."

PRINCIPLE
NUMBER IV

LOVE THEM
FIRST

Marcus thought for a minute then said, "All the principles seem to build on one another."

"Yes," replied Barnabas, "they build on one another to form something very special. But don't think for a moment that applying them comes naturally. In most cases, it's natural to do the opposite.

"We tend to take people for granted, instead of appreciating them. We are inclined to see and comment on their faults; we focus on their negative qualities instead of focusing on that which is positive about them. We also seem to find it easier to flex our power than to build our influence.

"And, as you have said today, we tend to want people to earn our respect instead of giving it to them from the outset."

Barnabas paused and then continued. "Marcus, these principles are not easily adopted. They do tend to go against our nature at times. We must first make a conscious decision to lead using the principles of the tablets. Then we must employ a sustained effort, but, as you apply the principles week after week, they become habit. Your level of respect with those you employ grows, and, with it, your ability to lead with influence grows."

With that said, each of the two men said their good-byes and left the shaded bench.

CHAPTER 12

An Environment to Thrive In

It started to storm that afternoon. Marcus and his crew went home. Despite Marcus's concern about the lost work time, it was nice to get home early and spend some time with his wife and girls. At dinner Arayliss asked, "Well, dear, what principle did you learn today?"

"Love them first," answered Marcus. Knowing this would not be enough, he went on to explain this principle to Arayliss as Barnabas had to him.

"I like it," said Arayliss. "It makes sense now that you explain it."

Marcus thought for a moment and said, "I knew Barnabas could help me, but I thought he would show me some tool or technique that he had. With these principles, instead of trying to come up with some bag of tricks that manipulate people to perform like you want, you actually create an environment in which people thrive."

"It sounds like you have been a very attentive student," said Arayliss.

CHAPTER 13

The Unifying Principle

If it weren't for the fast approaching deadline, Marcus would have really enjoyed the week. Mathis was now making daily visits to check on progress and constantly reminding Marcus of their agreement and its deadline. Even with Mathis's annoying visits, Marcus knew he had never worked in a better atmosphere. The new workers seemed happy and worked well with the rest of the crew. He watched as some true craftsmen were being born. The ship itself was fast becoming one of the finest in the harbor. All was going well until more rain came. And this time, once it started, it did not quit. Precious days were lost. Marcus felt helpless. The feeling of defeat was beginning to flare inside him.

Marcus awoke each day with hope that the rain had stopped. For five straight days, almost a whole, valuable week, it rained. When the rain finally stopped, the sun came out with a vengeance. It was hot and it was humid. But, Marcus and his crew weren't about to complain; they had five days to go and nine days of work left.

At the beginning of the week, Marcus called his men together explaining their situation. They all accepted the challenge before them and eagerly went to work. The day started out well. At noon, Marcus hated to leave, but he knew he must meet Barnabus and learn the principle of the last tablet. He was also in need of some supplies, so he left, promising to return soon.

Barnabus was waiting for him and immediately sensed Marcus's total concentration on his work. Marcus sat, and Barnabus spoke, "I saw Mathis, the ship agent, yesterday. He said you won't make your deadline."

Marcus shook his head, then replied, "I asked him for an extension, and he said the buyer refused. He said that a deal is a deal. But, that's all right because we are going to make it."

Barnabus smiled, patted Marcus on the leg and said, "I'm sure you will, son."

Marcus handed Barnabus tablet number four to be replaced in the small, old box. Barnabus removed the fifth and final tablet. "I know you are in a hurry, so I'll speak quickly." He handed Marcus the tablet.

PRINCIPLE NUMBER V

MAKE THEM FEEL THEY ARE PART OF SOMETHING SPECIAL

Marcus read principle number five aloud.

"Make them feel they are part of something special."

"Marcus, this principle is the glue that binds all the other four tablets together. If you can make your workers feel as if they are a part of something special, something greater than themselves, well, that's when miracles happen. Marcus, you have your goal. You have your challenge. Let them be part of it."

Barnabus stood, signaling the conversation was over. "I am traveling and am not sure when I shall return. I will be most anxious to see how all this turns out. I am proud of you, Marcus. You've been an excellent student."

"Thank you, Master," said Marcus. They hugged, and then both went their separate ways.

CHAPTER 14

Julius Steps Up

For the next few days, Marcus and his crew arrived before the sun rose and worked until the sunlight faded into darkness and they had to stop. The completion of the ship had become more than just a job. It was personal. Each man was determined not to be the reason for any delay. It was going to be close. The men were working skillfully and efficiently. It was easy now to appreciate and love them, if only he had just a little more time.

With two days to go, Marcus approached the men during their afternoon meal. "I want to thank all of you for all you have done," he said choking back tears. "I can't tell you how much it has meant to me to team up with such a fine group of men. We only have two days left and at least three or four days worth of work. Mathis, the ship agent, refuses to extend our contract. I was hoping to provide a bonus for you, but the penalty for missing our deadline will eliminate any profit on this ship. I just wanted to say thank you."

"Master, is there nothing we can do?" asked one of his workers.

"I'm afraid not," replied Marcus.

They finished their meal in silence. They resumed work in the hot humid sun. To Marcus's surprise, Julius disappeared for quite some time after the meal. When Julius returned and Marcus asked where he had gone, Julius just smiled and said, "You'll see." Marcus knew, for some reason, not to press the issue.

As darkness started to approach, people began to gather around the ship. Women, children, and what looked like other local workers appeared. Marcus paid little attention. Then a large ox-drawn cart pulled up and stopped next to the ship. Marcus looked at Julius as they both started walking toward the cart.

"What's this all about, Julius?"

Julius looked at Marcus. He smiled, then, winked, and said, "Help, Master, help."

"What good will all these people do? It's going to be dark soon and all the help in Athens won't matter if you can't see what you are doing."

Julius walked to the cart, pulled back the tarp and said, "That's what these are for." He reached in the wagon and took out two large torches. "The whole wagon is full of torches and lanterns. With these, Master, we will reach our goal. And with the help of our friends and family, we may even have some time to spare."

Marcus stood there too shocked to speak.

The men in the crowd made their way to the ship and started to work while the women and children, supervised by Arayliss, set up torches and prepared meals. Tents were raised with men rotating in and out, sleeping for a couple of hours then returning to work.

The shipbuilding became the talk of Athens. Shopkeepers, merchants, and townspeople sent supplies to help the hard-working men.

On the final day, Marcus had over one hundred men working nonstop. Several dozen workers were loaned by other shipbuilders. Everyone in Athens could feel the excitement.

On the final night, the night before the contract came due, Marcus did not sleep at all. He checked every inch of the ship. He was sure it was the finest ship he had ever seen. As the sun started to rise, he was confident all was done. He stood back and admired his fine ship. They did it, he thought, they did it!

He walked over to Julius and Arayliss who were eating by the fire. With tears forming in his eyes, he looked at them and said, "Thank you."

CHAPTER 15

Marcus Delivers the Ship to the New Owner

Marcus saw Mathis approaching from a distance. He had several men with him. One of them, Marcus guessed, was the new owner. As they approached, Marcus was surprised to see Barnabas with them.

"Have you completed the ship, Marcus?" asked Mathis.

"Yes. It is complete. You can send your inspectors aboard. I think you will find all is well."

Several hundred people had gathered around the ship. Everyone in Athens knew of the challenge the men had faced, and all were eager to see its outcome. Silence came over the crew and the crowd as they watched for the inspectors to return.

Finally, the inspectors came out and gave their nod of approval. The crowd cheered, and Marcus gave Arayliss a victory hug.

Barnabas who had stayed in the background approached Marcus and Mathis. He said, "Well done, my son."

"Thank you, Master." Marcus looked at Mathis and asked, "Does the new owner wish to take possession?"

"I don't know. Why don't you ask him yourself?" Mathis said, as he nodded at Barnabas.

Barnabas smiled at Marcus, who was suddenly confused.

"You're the owner?" he asked in disbelief.

Barnabas nodded in agreement.

"Master, why didn't you give me a couple more days or even a week? Why push so hard? Is building this ship so important?"

Barnabas put his arm around Marcus and said, "I wasn't thinking of building a ship. I was thinking of building a man!

"Do you remember the first day we met at the bench? We spoke of a wind. A wind that would move your ship, take you great places. A wind you needed to find."

"Yes, Master, I remember."

"That wind, my son, is leadership, the ability to lead others. Because of your application of the five principles of leadership that wind is no longer missing. You have become an excellent leader. I couldn't be more proud of you even if you were my own son."

Barnabas gave Marcus a bear hug and the crowd cheered again.

CHAPTER 16

Barnabas Invites Marcus to His Estate

Marcus slept for the next two days. When he finally got up, he went out and helped Arayliss in their garden. That day a messenger arrived and handed Marcus a letter. It asked him to come to Barnabas' estate that evening.

Marcus had never seen such a splendid house. Rich tapestry, marble floors, and columns that seemed to reach forever. He was led to an enclosed courtyard where Barnabas sat alone sipping wine.

"Greetings, Master," Marcus, said as he approached.

"Welcome, Marcus. How nice of you to come at such a short notice."

"Thank you for the invitation. It's always a pleasure to see you, Master."

"Marcus, I wish to speak with you. Please sit and drink some wine."

After sitting a while, Marcus asked something that had been on his mind, "Master, would you have really penalized me if I had missed my deadline?"

"Well, I never gave it much thought. You see, I knew you would make it. I never doubted it for a moment." Barnabas raised his cup for a toast. "To you, Marcus. You have learned well the five principles of leadership. If you continue to practice and apply them in your work and life, you will continue to be a great leader. I am certain of that."

"And to you, Master Barnabas," Marcus amended, "to a great leader and a great teacher."

Both drank deeply.

"Marcus, do you remember our original deal? We agreed I might ask you a favor at some time."

"Yes, of course, Master, I remember."

"Well, that time has come." Barnabas reached for the old wooden box that now contained all five clay tablets. He passed it to Marcus.

"These are the original tablets that were presented to me so many years ago. They are by far my most precious possession. I wish you to have them. Use them yourself and use them to teach the five principles to as many people as you can so their lives will become as wonderful as mine has been."

Finding it hard to speak, Marcus whispered, "I will do as you wish, Master."

"There will come a time, Marcus, when you too will pass the tablets on to someone else. You will know when that time comes, just as I know my time is now."

Marcus accepted the box with great care. "I shall do as you ask, Master."

"Splendid," replied Barnabas. He raised his cup again and said, "They will come in handy when you take over my entire operation next week."

CHAPTER 17

Practice the Principles

The five principles you have learned are building blocks you can use to make yourself a more effective leader. Just knowing the principles will not help you. You must practice and apply them to your life.

Instead of trying to apply them all at once, focus on one principle per week. Get several index cards. Write your weekly principle on a number of cards and place them all around your home and work. Keep the principle in front of you all day, reciting the principle every time you see it.

Repeat this process for all five principles. When you get to the end of the five principles, start over. Before you know it, a new style of leadership will emerge.

You will notice a wonderful change in your attitude and your people's attitudes.

When all five principles are learned and applied, you will receive the fruit of your effort, which will be a decrease in employee turnover, improved morale and productivity, and a better quality of life for all involved. Good luck and God bless you.

—Jack Myrick

THE
FIVE PRINCIPLES
OF LEADERSHIP

**I. MAKE THEM
FEEL APPRECIATED**

**II. SEE THEIR
POTENTIAL,
NOT THEIR FLAWS**

**III. LEAD WITH
INFLUENCE,
NOT POWER**

IV. LOVE THEM FIRST

**V. MAKE THEM FEEL
THEY ARE PART OF
SOMETHING SPECIAL**

Five-Week Action Plan

BEFORE YOU START

Make a list of the five to seven people who have the most impact on your success and your stress. They can be people that work for you. Maybe you work for them, or perhaps they're a teammate. They are the people who impact your present and your future in a positive way the most. I call them your CORE.

1. _____

2. _____

3. _____

4. _____

5. _____

Now rate where your relationship is with that person from 1–5; With 5 being great to 1 being very poor. The goal is simple here. These people on your CORE have a tremendous impact on your life, so you must be very intentional about these relationships.

I'm not saying you ignore the other relationships in your life, but rather be very intentional about where you invest your time and energy. Your CORE relationships are the ones that impact you the most, so don't put them on auto pilot. Be intentional.

WEEK #1
Make them feel appreciated

A wise man recently said, "Appreciation is the currency of the future."

During week one, spend some time reflecting on your CORE List. Do the people on that list *Feel Appreciated?* What have you done to give them that feeling? There's a good chance several people on your list are some of your top performers. Unfortunately those are the exact people we often take for granted. We know they do a great job and we get used to it. We stop commenting on their work and accomplishments. Please get back in the habit of recognizing them. Help them understand how valuable they really are to you.

There may be others on your list where the relationship is possibly strained right now. Look for the positive traits in them and acknowledge them. This will go a long way to restoring the relationship. A great formula when expressing your appreciation is: ***WHAT-WHEN-HOW***:

1. **What they did.** The specific behavior or accomplishment.

2. **When they did it.** Again be specific here.

3. **How it affected you.** Use feeling words

Here's an example: Sam when you turned in your part of the report early yesterday, it made my job so much easier. I'm truly blessed to have you on the team.

It's short, simple and powerful.

What they did, when they did it, how it affected you.

Remember there are **three characteristics of effective appreciation:**

1. It has to be **REAL and GENUINE**.

2. It is **SPECIFIC.** What they did. How they did it and how that positively impacted you and others.

3. **It is CONSISTENT.** It's not a behavior you have for special occasions.

Which relationship from your CORE needs to be worked on?

If the people around you truly felt valued and appreciated what would happen to their productivity?

Don't leave this principle to random chance. How can you create a system to remind you do this consistently?

How can you use tools to remind you to appreciate those around you, like Outlook, Text Minder App, index cards, etc.?

How can you appreciate the little things that people around you do?

Please make sure to use this principle with family.

List three things *You Will Do* to make people around you feel valued and appreciated.

1. _____

2. _____

3. _____

WEEK #2
See their potential not their flaws

It seems like we're hardwired to notice the negative. I managed restaurants for over thirty years. Because of my training I can walk into any restaurant, not even one of mine, and spot a thousand things needing improvement.

What's funny is that I also, at the same instant, see a thousand things going right. Where do you think my brain focuses? The negative! I truly notice the good stuff, but my brain wants desperately to dwell on the things not going well.

It's the same with people. It seems their negative behaviors scream at us and we have to mine hard for the positive ones. A cool thing about leading people over a long period of time is you get a chance to see people develop to their full potential as their career progresses. You get to see their development from beginning to end.

It's often easier for me to connect the dots to their success better than they can themselves. As a good leader it's my responsibility to communicate their potential. By doing this we can help them see them become the best version of themselves.

Where did someone in your past help you see your true potential?

How did that inspire you?

As you look at the people on your team, list three things about each person that you see as strengths that adds value to the team.

How can you communicate to a team member what you see as real potential?

How can you help believe it too?

What does it do for someone when they understand that a person in authority sees real potential in them?

List three things *You Will Do* to communicate your people's potential this week.

1. _____

2. _____

3. _____

WEEK #3
Lead with influence, not power

Leading with influence means that as a leader you have created an environment where your team is engaged and doesn't have to be monitored constantly. The relationship with one's direct report is probably the most influential relationship in an organization. The biggest lever for employee engagement is this relationship. Manage it wisely.

Explain how I can gain more influence with those I lead.

How would you describe your leadership style now, influence or power?

If people are doing things only because they have to, how can I increase my influence with them?

Define ways bosses who lead with power actually discourage employees from working harder?

List three things *You Will Do* to increase your influence with your team this week.

1. _____

2. _____

3. _____

WEEK #4
Love them first

When we talk about love here, we are talking about what the Greeks would call agape love. It is described as unconditional, respectful.

I would define love in this context as giving them my respect and encouragement up front. They don't have to earn it.

Where have you been prejudging people?

Where have you made it hard to connect because preconceived ideas or expectations?

How will you deal with the inevitable disappointments when you love first?

Why is it easier for people to connect with you when you *Love Them First?*

Leadership is about people. If you don't love people, leadership will always be hard and stressful for you.

List three things *You Will Do* to show love to your people.

1. _____

2. _____

3. _____

WEEK #5
Make them feel they are a part of something special

People today want to feel what they do matters. Some companies are naturally equipped with their missions because what they do clearly serves the community with some higher purpose. Other organizations have to look a little deeper.

When I was managing restaurants it wasn't much of a mission to sell hamburgers. I couldn't sell the idea we were changing the world by putting burgers in a bag. What I could sell was it wasn't just a place to work, but a place to belong.

When you worked for me you were joining our family. We created a family environment. People all over our communities are searching to belong. We gave them a place to belong. I made them feel a part of something special, part of a family.

As a result, our turnover was a fraction of our competitors.

What can you do to make those who you work with *feel a part of something special?*

What's so special about working on your team?

How can making them feel valued give them a feeling of being a part of something special?

List three things *You Will Do* to help your people feel a part of something special.

1. _____

2. _____

3. _____

REPEAT THE PROCESS

I recently had a conversation with a doctor who had just read The Shipbuilder. She told me she tried it and it didn't work. She was seeing the principles like a vaccination. One shot and it's done.

I told her it wasn't like that at all. It was more like bathing. It wasn't a onetime fix. It's a habit that needs to be done consistently.

There is no guaranteed time frame before you will see some great results. It's like most important accomplishments we achieve in our life; they're accomplished little by little over a period of time.

You've heard of the Golden Rule: "Treat people like you wish to be treated".

So how would you like to have a leader that:

- Really makes you feel valued and appreciated.

- Sees your potential and communicates it to you frequently.

- Influences you so you want to do a great job.

- Cares about you unconditionally as a person.

- Makes you feel like you a part of something special.

Wouldn't it be awesome to have a leader like that!

Let me tell you a secret. The only thing better than having a leader like that is being a leader like that.

Enjoy the journey.

—Jack

Help others to benefit from the five principles of leadership. Share this book with a friend or coworker.

ABOUT THE AUTHOR

During a very difficult, low point in his business career, Jack Myrick found himself looking at those working with him and blaming them for his circumstances. He thought, "If they would just do their jobs like they were supposed to then I wouldn't be in this situation."

At the end of his rope, Jack took some time off for reflection.

By stepping back and looking at his situation he realized he had two choices: either quit and find a new career or change. By being totally honest with himself, he discovered that before his circumstances could change, he had to change.

Jack began to ask himself, "What kind of leader could turn this situation around?" He then developed some simple leadership principles, as well as strategies on how to implement them. The effect was so dramatic for him, he knew he had to share them with others in *The Shipbuilder*.

The principles of *The Shipbuilder* work because they tap into the innermost needs and desires of those we lead. They inspire. They help us connect. Apply them today and you too will discover a wonderful transformation.

Jack Myrick is president and founder of Management Solutions, a management training company, as well as head of Myrick Enterprises, a restaurant development group. He lives in Central Oklahoma and is blessed with a wonderful wife and three incredible daughters.

You can contact Jack Myrick at
jack@publicstrategies.com.

The Shipbuilder Services

Speakers: Experience an inspiring and powerful program that presents The Shipbuilder principles and offers strategies on how to apply them.

Workshops: Bring the skills for change directly to your people. This in-depth training is a fun, informative four-hour workshop based on the five leadership principles of *The Shipbuilder*. Each workshop attendee receives a hardcover copy of *The Shipbuilder*, a *Shipbuilder* workbook, and a lifetime's worth of leadership tools.

Jack Myrick's presentations and workshops are known for their Southern charm and practicality.

For information, please call
(405) 848-2171
or email jack@publicstrategies.com

Share the benefits of the five principles of leadership with a friend or coworker

To order individual copies of this book, please telephone
Quill Driver Books at 1-800-345-4447 or visit QuillDriverBooks.com.

For details on bulk quantity purchases for premiums, sales promotion,
employee training programs, or fundraisers,
call 1-800-345-4447 or email Info@QuillDriverBooks.com.

Did this book help you?
We'd love to hear how you put this book to
work for yourself and/or your organization.

Email us at jack@publicstrategies.com

Printed in the USA
CPSIA information can be obtained
at www.ICGtesting.com
JSHW082223140824
68134JS00015B/710